CATHARSIS

Paige Hart
&
Jack Boad

Mostly, for our family and friends.
But also for everyone who said we could do it and
everyone, including us, who thought that we couldn't.

And if you find yourself wondering if one of these
poems was written about you, it likely was.

* Middle Finger Emoji *

My head is overflowing
Flooded with stories
And I am desperate for the
dam to burst
To let them pour
With every breath
I take

With a pencil to my temple
A game of Russian roulette
begins
The risk is my rush
The reward is the clarity that
follows
This isn't just poetry
I am performing
Brain surgery
Letting the trapped words
Pour into the basin beside me
Finally free
To fill up the pages

My heart aches with
Buried pain
Beating hard and fast
As it reminds me that
This is real
And I am real
But now it's time to let go
Send the elevator back down
To pick up somebody else
Who needs this ride

With a hand on my chest
I feel the beat
The music of my life
Pulsing just below my skin
This isn't just poetry
I am performing
Heart surgery
Removing the growth
That trauma left behind
And stitching the wound
tightly

To give it a chance to heal

Silent and alone
I let it pour
From my head and heart
Into ink and paper
A release I so desperately
need

A therapy I can finally feel
Something I can give myself
Whenever the strain of it all
Gets too much

This is my beginning
This is my catharsis

Brain surgery

Maybe it was the black cat
Who's path I crossed
Maybe it was the ladder
That I absentmindedly walked
under
Or it could have been the
cracks
In the pavement
That I decided to step on
Again and again
And again
Like pressing piano keys
Whatever it is, it has me
feeling like
I'm being slowly sucked
Into a black hole
Where nothing could possibly
survive
And everything is darkness
No sound
No light
No hope
The only chance I have is to
Hang on for dear life
As the forces pull at my feet
Trying their best to drag me
Down
Into the void
That I've desperately tried
To avoid
Sharp thoughts stab me
Why do I deserve this, now?
What bad decision did I
make?
What wrong turn did I take?
I grab at anything that I can
But my grip always slips
And this time, I give in
I scream but it's no good
It has me now
And there I float
In nothing but darkness
Trapped, alone

Whilst time passes slowly
around me
With no choice but to accept
my fate
Perhaps it's not so bad,
Peaceful even
At least it will be over
And I can make peace with it
As more time passes
I feel less aware
Perhaps this was what I was
looking for
An escape route
Or perhaps this time
I really am just gone

Bong
Another news story fills the screen
What will it be today?
A bomb scare,
A murder,
A tsunami,
A hurricane?
Whatever it is you can guarantee it won't be
An easy watch

Bong
Tonight's main story
"Something fucking dreadful"
Because the world is a morbid place
Misery loves company
And fear sells a hell of a lot better
Than happiness does

Bong
Thousands dead
Millions injured
Billions left in squalor
Everyone is left completely numb
And nobody is immune

Bong
That's it for the latest terror review
Join us tomorrow for more of the same
It never gets better
Only worse
Because in this twisted reality
We hate the idea of happily ever after
And so nothing will ever change

Deep down inside me
It lingers
Something menacing and
cruel
Prowling around restlessly
Waiting to rear its ugly head
*You know I'm down here,
unleash me!*
Desperately trying to make
Something of myself
I have now become
Unhinged
The pursuit of power
The desperation to be
remembered
Is ironic when
I can't even remember who I
am
Anymore
I have started talking to
myself
*First sign of madness, mad
man*
Writhing and screaming
Certifiably insane
Utterly bonkers
More power!
Ha ha ha ha ha ha ha!
Around me electricity pulses
Crackling dangerously
It tickles
As another switch is flipped
I stumble
Wary of the danger
Is it really worth the cost?
You'll be my best creation yet
*I'll be the fucking death of
you*
Lights flash
Warning's scream
Beeps and boops
Science meets jazz

Skeeeepppbittttybboopppboo
pppbadoo
And outside the thunder roars
Lightning
Flashes of my silhouette
Windows rattle with the
power
Of a tormented sky
Time to pull the final lever
Just pull the fucking lever!
Power surges and I am on fire
The monster inside is
unleashed
And it is everything we'd
hoped for
Let's burn the fucking world
together

Yes, let's.

A red-hot poker
Burns into the back of my brain
Constantly
Fuelling the need
Feeding the want
Driving the senseless desire
It requires unwavering attention
But still my body trembles
With the effort it takes to stop myself
From tipping the scales
From obsession, to addiction, to oblivion
Losing balance
Boundaries blurring
I can't shake it
Instead I crave it
Unsure if I ever want it to stop

This morning at
Precisely 9.05am
I saw a guy drunk already
On a bench,
Alone in the park,
And I felt for him
Because I know how it feels
To have one too many reasons
To numb life
In whatever way you can

It's strange to look into
A mirror like that

People think that having
Anxiety means that we just get
Worried and fearful about life's non-issues
Overreact to everything for attention
Lose it at anything just for the sake of it
When in reality, anxiety is that feeling you get
When your chair is about to tip backwards
Or when you miss a step as you're
Climbing the stairs
Over and over
They don't understand the sheer
Embarrassment and frustration
When you can't cross a road alone
Or make a call
Or go your own way
It isn't a feeling of worry,
Or a desperate need for attention
It's another sleepless night because of your own
Irrational brain
Another tight chested feeling that something bad is
Waiting around every single corner
But no matter how many times people tell you
You're wrong,
Or being silly
You won't believe it
Not for a second
And even though it hurts you to hear it
You still hope that they never have to feel it

I didn't feel it at all
As you burrowed your way
Deep inside my brain
You set up shop
And poisoned my thoughts
Blissfully unaware
I was completely unsuspecting
I was ignorant
Until it was far too late

Now here we are together
Me and you, the parasite
That always lives inside my brain
Wriggling into
Everything I do
Every thought
Every decision
Every action
One day I'll be rid of you
Even if it means
Cutting you out myself

Bad days.
Often they jump out at you when you're
least expecting it. Other times they creep in
slowly. Like a shadow. You don't notice it
looming over you until you're caught inside it.
Bad days make me wonder, what's the fucking
point of it all? Am I a hamster trapped in its
wheel for five days a week, running the same
constant loop? When I finally get off I'm too
dizzy to think straight. You're supposed to be
grateful for the opportunity, right? For the
pleasure of mundanity.
Eat. Sleep. Work. Repeat.
Some days I'm not interested in being grateful
to the man. I'm not bothered about making them
more money whilst I make the same. For all I
know the sun might be shining outside, the
birds might be singing, too. Everyone else clambers
over each other to soak it up on their
designated breaks but I can't find the energy
to bother. Burnt out and tired. The comfort of
my own bed calls to me and who am I to resit
it? So I draw the curtains, close my eyes and think,
fuck today.

My leg won't stop
Incessantly bouncing
Pieces of split skin
Surround my fingertips
Left red, sore and bloody
From the biting
I can never seem to stop the
biting
My entire body is slumped
Buckling from the weight of
my own
Assumptions
Shoulders arched
Elbows digging sharply
Into my knees
Leaving red patches
As another reminder of just
how long it has been

I slap my cheeks
A rhythm for encouragement
Giving myself a stern word
I try to shake off the dread
Instead the echoes of self-
doubt
Fill my mind
Coming from a place
That I don't really understand
But is somehow always
present
I am swallowed whole, lost
In its shadow
Constantly cold and cowering
Even on the good days
The sun can't keep me warm

An escape
That's all I'm searching for
An end to the constant cycle
Of anxious moments
A miserable roller coaster ride
Stuck before the big drop
Waiting for an answer

To a mundane question
That makes me sweat
And panic
Overwhelmed by a
Desire to unplug, switch off
and
Disconnect
A desperate attempt to push
away
The familiar lonely pinch of
despair
When the replies don't come
fast enough
Or even at all
Defeated and deflated
I close my laptop
Turn off my phone
Close the curtains
Close myself from the world
So I can't be seen as
vulnerable
And so that I can't see what's
left outside
Whilst I waste away, waiting

There is a feeling I have,
A brief second
When I am
Completely
Overcome with a desperation
To do the worst possible thing
That my brain can think of
The direct opposite of what I
should
It's not an urge
But a re-enforcement
Of the right choice
To not take the plunge and
Enter the void
Sometimes I find myself
On a road, driving
Oncoming headlights
Almost blinding and I could
Very easily
Swerve and
Steer into the void
Standing on
A bridge
Looking down into the abyss
It would be so easy to let
myself
Jump into the void
Waiting for a train
The next one isn't due to stop
Feeling the vibrations
I am tempted to grab hold
As it thunders past me
Pulled into the void
A flame burns bright
From a candle
And my hand hovers
longingly
Above
Desiring to feel the heat
Melt into the void
I don't act
I don't harm
I don't end it all

But sometimes there are
moments
When sat upon my shoulder is
The Imp of the Perverse
Whispering into my ear
Goading me into doing
something awful
Basking in that split second
when I consider it
The sweet release
I would find
Safe within the void

Do you ever just
Zone out
For a while
Your eyes lose focus
Your ears go deaf
And your mind completely blanks
Until you can barely feel anything more
Than the air around you
And the steady rise and fall
Of your chest
Your brain nothing more than
An old TV full of static
Covered in dust
The world nothing more than
White noise
And so I sit
Or lay
Or stand
I'm not sure
I'm entirely disconnected
From the nonsense
For so long that when I do return
I can't remember how I started
It takes a while for me to remember
Where I am
And who I am
And in those brief seconds
Before realisation hits
I do not feel afraid
Or lonely
Just content at the thought
Of being nothing more than another part
Of nature
Connected to the real world
For a brief, fleeting moment
Floating on the wind

Hot water rains down
And now after another long day
My mind can finally wander
Skipping past my regular thoughts
Once again full
Of too much stress and worry
Ending up in whatever the hell this part is
A weird and wonderful wonderland
And I can't help but wonder

Would ducks look better wearing armour?
And why does Wednesday feel like an odd number?
Isn't sleeping just a form of time travel?
And why is moist such an unpleasant sounding word?
If animals could talk, what would be the rudest animal?
How many chicken nuggets would be too many chicken nuggets?
Why do I have fingertips, not toe tips, but I can tip toe?
Why are buildings called buildings when they're built?

And while we're here...
Isn't it scary to think that we're on a planet that's propelling at such an
alarming rate whilst rotating round a giant sun shaped bomb and we
very rarely take the time to stop and take in our surroundings, often
missing out on the little things because we're too busy glued to our
screens to notice there is a world out there just waiting to be explored
and before we know it we're not going to have the time to explore it
and... BOOM! We're toast.
.
.
.
.

.
And also, when you think about it
Isn't cheese just a loaf of milk?

I was stuck inside a maze
With no idea how to find my way
Back home again
The walls were so tall and thick
That I had no way of knowing the difference
Between where I was going
And where I'd been
Each painstaking twist and turn led me to
Another place that I was so sure
I had seen before
With every familiar dead end
Came another wave of panic
Eventually after so much lost time
I stood just metres
From the exit
I tried to run but didn't know
That you'd already tied my laces together
And I hit the ground to the sound
Of your vicious laughter
I raised my head just in time to see
The exit wasn't a way out at all
It was only a mirage
And then the realisation slowly began to set in
That I wasn't caught in a maze at all
But in-fact a spider's web
And somehow, I was the fly

That fucking alarm
Everyday
Beep beep beep beep beep beep
Beep beep be..
I smash my hand down
Rolling over with a deep sigh
And blurred eyes
Making the noises of someone much older
As I try to get up in one smooth motion
Whilst my body begs me to lay back down
I throw on my dressing gown
Slip into my slippers and realise that
Both need a good wash
Slowly I make my way to the stairs
And start my decent
Carefully does it
I'm still half asleep
Wishing I was still dreaming

Downstairs it's cold in the kitchen
The sound of the kettle boiling
Fills the silence around me
Keeping me awake
I scoop some cheap instant coffee
Into a giant mug
Hoping that it's big enough to give me the boost I need
To face another day

I'm careful
Not to burn the coffee
Or my hand
I leave it black
And take a big sniff
That familiar morning aroma
That tells me it's time to put on another brave face
Outside there is frost on the grass
Somewhere close by a robin is chirping away
I light up a cigarette
Enjoying some heat from the lighter
And take that first drag
Exhaling with a sigh
Another fucking day in paradise

My entire body burns
As I stand outside
In the pouring rain
The pressure of everything
Closing in around me
I can hear it sizzling
Instead of splashing
And the smell of sulphur burns my nostrils
With every sharp inhale
My eyes are blood red
And my skin is pink
The treetops are dead
The soil is dead
Everything is being eaten away
In front of my own eyes
All that is left is a dull, empty void
I look up at the shrivelled remains
Of the forest around me
And I somehow see your face
In the withered branches
Wearing the same old expression you always had
It's haunting but somehow
Fitting
That I see it again now
Amongst all this destruction
There is nothing left
But emptiness
All the animals have run to safety
The birds have flown away
And I am left standing here alone
Burning in a downpour of acid rain
Waiting to melt away

A sudden and aggressive
Bright, blinding light
Bursts through my window
With such a force it
Slams them open
And leaves the curtains
flapping
I shoot up in bed
Immediately alert
Eyes wide
Hair standing
Teeth on edge
I can't move
I can't hear
All I can do is watch the
whirling set
Of small, pretty lights
Dancing right in front of me
Before I can react
My pupils dilate
And my body becomes
lifeless
I begin to float
Am I dreaming?
Am I dead?
As I'm pulled towards the
window
Something calls to me
Something calming
The lights get brighter
And brighter
And brighter
Until I am blinded completely
Just as it becomes too much
to bear
Everything zaps
Into nothing
And I wake up
Cold, naked,
Lost and alone
Surrounded by thick trees
Surprisingly I feel calm
And somewhat grateful

My breath hangs in the chilly
air
In front of me
And I look up
To see one final flash into the
nights sky
Before it disappears
completely
Leaving me with only
A picture of stars and frosty
treetops
A fleeting visit
But what does it all mean?

A ballroom overflowing with friends
Shouldn't make me feel
Like I'm alone, stuck in a trap
Surrounded by strangers
Sometimes even enemies
The familiar, friendly faces are hard to focus on when
I'm under the influence
To numb the experience
And they're all under the influence too
But with a difference
They are being transformed within the
Candlelight
As they dance and dance
Completely carefree and oblivious
To the sad sight of me
Stood on the side-lines
Suffering in silence
As the deafeningly loud room overwhelms me
Everybody else in the room is
Connected
But they can't feel my loose connection
For them, the room is colourful
And warm
They can't see how grey my corner is
So here I stand
A spectator
Watching the world go by in front of me
Lonely and silent
In the darkest corner of the brightest room
Unable to join in the fun because
Nobody puts me in the corner
But me

I am the load
Sitting upon your shoulders
That you desperately try to carry
With you every single day
But I am so unbearably heavy
That it bends your back
Almost to breaking point
Slowly forcing you down
Towards the ground
Until eventually you have no choice but to
Lay flat, exhausted
Being crushed beneath the force of me
Pushing your face into cold concrete slabs
Small pieces of stone
Cut into your cheeks
I'm relentless
Squeezing the life out of you
I am your worst headache
I am your biggest worry
I am the reason
For your fear, sadness and stress
I am your burden
And you will never get rid of me

For a while I collected up
All my unused wishes
Saving them for one big wish
When the time was right
I turned from every 11:11
Kept every eyelash that I could have blown away
Pocketed every coin not flipped into a fountain
And for every candle blown out
I kept my mind completely empty
So that I could keep them all
Locked inside a box
Safe and sound
Buried deep
Living without the fear
That a runaway want
Would creep up on me
And waste them all
Without a second thought

As time went by
I bided my time
Until finally
I knew what I wanted
And it was time to trade
But my heart broke
As I found my box was empty
All my wishes had escaped
Without me even noticing
They must have known
They must have understood
Exactly what I'd been waiting for
What I'd been saving them for
Because they'd gone ahead and
Spent themselves on you
Beautiful and calm
Holding my pile of wishes in your hands
Everything I needed
Brought together

A reflection stares back
That I almost do not recognise
A young face
No tell-tale lines of stress
No bags under the eyes
A genuine smile
And an innocent expression
Full of hope and happiness
It looks back at the real me
Stood alone in an unlit room
Tired and in desperate need
Of a decent rest
They are complete polar opposites

An older face
With all the tell-tale lines of stress
Dark circles under the eyes
And a mouth turned downwards, frowning
With the look of somebody
Who has seen it all
And hates what they've seen
But continues on
Hoping something, someday
Might change

One thinks they're seeing their future
The other, their past
They both offer a hand
Pressing their palm down on the cold glass
Understanding, but confused
Who's to say what's real
And what's imaginary
In our darkest days
Or what's just a simple memory
Trapped inside a mirror
Reminding us of what we were
Before
Or what might be waiting for us

I've been simply surviving
For so long now
That I'm struggling to remember the last time
I actually lived
Instead of finding myself
Staring down the barrel
Of yet another bottle
Because I can't afford a gun
Looking for any golden sips
That might be hiding at the bottom
Sliding another Marlboro out the pack
The flame provides the only light
To this otherwise darkened room
I try to imagine past conversations
Going back and forth over old ground
Neither giving up an inch
And I can't help but wonder
What could have been different
If I'd only dropped my guard
Or if I could have just tried harder
I was one decision away
From a totally different life
But the finish line just kept moving
Even now, after everything
I couldn't change a thing
And I'll never be able to

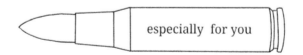

especially for you

There was a time
When I found myself
Completely and utterly
Powerless
Whilst you had it all
A looming shadow that stood
tall
Over me
Blocking out the sunlight
Every single day
I shivered
Whilst cowering in the shade
Searching for any way out
Any crack I could wriggle out
of
A slither of hope
I could prise apart

One day I finally found one
And decided that
This was it
I'd had enough
I dug deep within myself
Until I found the strength
To finally fight back
Standing in your face
I was no longer afraid or
willing to
Let you step on me
The shock of my rebellion
Kept you frozen in place just
long enough
For me to have the last word
And in the blink of on an eye
I broke you
Your cold, sharp pieces
Came crashing down all
around me
Shattered by my courage,
Shattered by the sheer force
of
Me
And the strength of those
around me

Who love me enough
To stand by my side
As I take back the power that
you stole
From inside of me
And place it back
In my own hands
Refusing to ever be that
vulnerable
Again

My brain works in odd ways
Sometimes
One moment
There is nothing but clarity
And tranquillity
I can sit and think about
Calm ocean waves
And see the facts
Laid out in front of me
For exactly what they are
But before I know it
My brain has flipped
Throwing everything up in the air
And everything I know
Feels like fiction
This story of my life
Unravelling
Because fiction isn't real
Yet often it feels like it is
And I have to remind myself that once again
This is make believe
If only I could make up my fucking mind
About what's real and
What's not
A double-edged sword
That can flip
And slice
And cut
Until the calm ocean waves
Turn into a storm
And I have no choice but to watch
Mesmerised
An experience stranger than fiction
And equally as dangerous

She was finally feeling it
I think, for the first time
Those big, beautiful blues of hers
Suddenly engulfed in black
It'll never feel this good for her again
Chemicals mixing in her brain
Are absorbing her reality
She feels it
Happily submits to it
And dances
Into an alternate universe

The exact moment I allowed myself
To leave my thoughts behind
And shut my eyes
I embarked upon a journey
Somewhere beyond the stars
I flew between planets
Waved to all the creatures
And enjoyed a spin around the rings of Saturn
1.4925 billion km from home
(At the time, anyway)

For a while, I was an explorer
But when I finally returned
I found myself back in my own bed
Feeling too far away
From the stars and planets
I'd called my friends
All too soon
I had crash landed
Back on this rock we call Earth
Wishing for the day to end
So that I can dream of something cosmic

A mile high
You're circling
Your laser sharp vision
Looking down on me
Just gliding on the breeze
Waiting patiently
For the perfect chance
To catch me off guard
And strike
I'll never see it coming
Look at me
Eyes glued to the ground
Unaware you're overhead
Scavenging and searching
Looking for your next meal
Completely oblivious
That it's me

Bleak walls shine
Like only cheap paint can
A terrible, sickening yellow
Who decided this would be a good choice?
Perhaps it's supposed to represent the sun?
But all it manages to do
Is serve as a reminder that in fact
I'm trapped
This room feels like a nightmare
It drenches me in confusion
With its dusty tables
Leaking ceilings
And dirty, coffee-stained carpets
It is starting to feel like
You can no longer pay me enough to be here
And the expressionless, defeated faces
Sitting around me
Empty, except for nothing at all
Tapping away on cheap plastic keyboards
Like mindless robots
Only tells me what I already know
I have to find a way out
This cannot be my future

Late nights turn into
Early mornings
Without a moments sleep
Because the wire is too busy zapping
A current that never stops
And here I lay exhausted
But unable to push aside the thoughts
That plague me
It's like being continuously
Punched in the head
Bruising my mind
Over and over until
I am nothing more
Than a venomous snake
Shaking my tail
Baring my fangs
Waiting for my chance to strike
At the first unlucky passer by
Who tries to handle me
Because fuck them for getting involved
I struggle to shed this skin
A difficult trait I cannot change,
Will not change
Why should I have to fucking change?
Because I am charging through regardless
The choice is yours
Get out of my way
Or get fucking bitten!

An empty whisky bottle
Rolls gently across the wooden floor
Making an all too familiar sound
Stopping eventually when it reaches
The table leg
With a clink
The other empty bottles sit
Upon the tabletop
Looking down at their fallen brother
Surrounded by their own
Spills
Slumped at the table is a
Miserable creature
Full of pain
Moaning about how once again
The glass is empty
Unsteadily it tries to stand
To find another bottle
The room spins
And its feet go from under it
So it falls
Crashing to the floor
And there it stays
Drunk
Blurry eyes finally close
The empty bottle
The last thing it sees before giving in
To sleeping on the floor
Like it did the night before
And even, the night before that
A monster
Stuck at the bottom of a hole
It drank itself into

A deafening silence
Pounds inside my head
Grasping for words that remain unsaid
On my tongue they sit, primed
Ready to tumble out
Instead they stay stuck in place
And I sit
Stone faced and still
Trapped inside my thoughts
Desperate for a different perspective
Desperate for some other way to feel
But only ever finding the familiar feeling,
Of feeling forgotten
So again, I'm clinging on
Struggling to stay afloat
Breathless and tired
My throat burns with words still trapped inside
I wonder
Is anybody there

To pull them out?

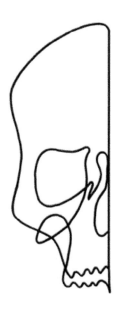

Why is it so easy
And almost completely natural
To watch everybody else
And think they're doing
So much better than you are
With their never-ending stream of
Exciting status updates
Over filtered photographs,
Fake teeth, fake eyebrows, fake tans
All posted to remind you that
You are doing absolutely nothing
While they thrive
On their patch of grass
That is far greener than yours is
I bet it doesn't even need mowing
And they look very happy with themselves
Don't they?
That is until you remember
That you are in the real world
And all of a sudden
You find that your own patch isn't so bad
After all
Because it's real
Even when it's raining,
At the very least
It's real

Shiny, happy people
Are everywhere I look
With big, wide smiles
Plastered across their faces
Always without even a hint of
a crack
Leaving me filled with equal
parts
Jealously, anger and
Admiration
As I wear the crack riddled
smile
That I painted on
This morning
The same as every morning
Using a mirror and some
makeup
Meant for a clown
I do my best to make it stick
But it continuously threatens
to slip
Every time I dare to
Take a breath
And I wonder
How do they do it?
Perhaps their smiles are as
fake as mine
And they're just better actors
than I am
Maybe I will find my own
One day
Until then I'll keep applying
the makeup
Painstakingly
Every
Single
Fucking exhausting
Morning
Keeping my movements to a
minimum
So it doesn't slip

And expose my blank
expression
Pushing forward as much as I
can
Until I can throw the makeup
away
For good
No longer needing a mask
Because I will finally be able
to smile
Without one

I had forgotten how it felt
To live in technicolour
For far too long I'd let the world
Slowly drain away
All of the colour around me
Going down the sink
Until all I was left with
Was a monochrome nightmare
Leached of anything original
Or fun
But one day in the distance
I spotted a trail,
A tiny splash of colour
And then another
As if they'd been left behind by someone
Immune to the mundanity I was used to
And suddenly I could see the splashes
Everywhere
More and more until
My surroundings were reinvented at last
Even better than before
Now I am forever grateful
To that person
Whoever they were
For removing the grayscale filter
From my eyes
And reminding me
Just how colourful
Life can be

"Always let your conscience be your guide"
That's what we're always told
A simple set of words designed
To keep us on the straight and narrow
And, most of the time
I can get onboard with that
Plain sailing through life
Knowing right from wrong
Making the odd mistake, sure
But that's to be expected, right?
But it begs the question,
What if your moral compass is way off?
What then?
For the most part I am in control
But I'd be lying if I said
That the devil sat upon my shoulder
Doesn't sometimes shout louder
Than the angel on the other
I'd also be lying if I was to say
That there wasn't a part of me that likes it
After all, that devil can be mighty charming
And that angel can be a right bore
And me?
Well I'm just there in the middle
Stuck between a rock and a hard place
Usually trying to do my best
But enjoying my occasional worst

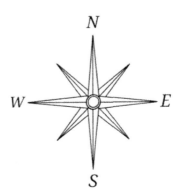

When your mind can't take any more trauma - it's only natural that your heart is next to break.

Heart surgery

All I've ever wanted
Is to be one piece
Of the little puzzle
That is your life

Whether it fits or not.

I am full of soft sighs
I am full of you
I am defined by my trembles
Trembles in my knees, hands and voice
The inevitable 4am conversations when
Our tongues are drunk and honest

I am full of the idea of your hands
On my skin

I am full of poetry that I don't know
How to write
Poetry about how your lips curve up
At the edges when you're telling a joke
And how your eyes sparkle from
Dawn till dusk

I am full of the idea that love can
Conquer anything and if a god can love
A mortal: why can't I believe in the
Idea that you could love me

The same way that I love you

I never understood what it meant
To be whole
To find that thing
That person
That would fit me
Exactly
I was a puzzle
Unaware that a piece was missing
Until you came into my life
And like a square peg in a square hole
You completed the scene
Now here we are
Tangled within each other's
Heartstrings
A beautiful chaos
Intertwined by our
Thoughts and feelings
Fears and loves
Ups and downs
And our dreams
Impossible to break free
Even if we wanted to
The sharpest knife
Couldn't cut through
The strongest will
Couldn't pull us apart
We are living and breathing as one
How lucky we are
To have found a respite
Within each other
As the world around us
Crumbles and dies

I wonder if you felt it
The first time we met
Because my heart hit the floor
With a thud that rattled my
bones
I never saw it coming
But I welcomed the shock
As it jarred my teeth

I wonder if you knew
As I did, there and then
That there would be no way
of
Walking away from this one
Because just like that
In the blink of an eye
My heart
Belonged to you
It was ripped off my sleeve
And you put it in your pocket
All you really did was smile
And I was yours

I wonder if you knew
How happy you made me
How content I was
And how everyday was a
good day
Until it wasn't

I wonder if you cared
That when you packed your
bags
And snuck away
Whilst I was working
That you were leaving me
Trapped within that feeling
you get
In between tripping
And catching yourself
When your chest jolts
And your breath catches

Because you're so sure you're
going to fall
Flat on your face

I wonder if you considered
me
And walked away anyway
Without a reason
Without a goodbye
And now I lay awake at night
Struggling to breathe
Wondering about you
As I learn to stand on my own
two feet
All over again

I have a tendency
To feel too deeply
And meeting you
Was no exception
The first time you smiled
I was hooked
Now every time I look at you
My pupils dilate
Almost like my eyes are trying
To see as much of you as possible
The fire
Has fused us together
A chemical reaction
That neither of us can stop
And it feels dangerous
Like we could combust at any moment
Wiping out anything in our way

I was used to living
Just above the water
Breathing easily
Basking in the sun
Just existing
Until suddenly
Something grabbed a hold of my ankles
And slowly began to pull me under
With my legs bound it was impossible
To tread water and stay
Afloat
Chest tight with panic
I floundered
Lungs burning
Mouth full of water
I began to
Drown
Completely submerged
I sank
Lower and lower
I could no longer breathe at all
Until a figure above
Broke through the surface
Fragments of sunlight glimmered
And there you were
Holding me
Until the grip on my ankles loosened
And disappeared
You pulled me to the shore
Beat the life back into my chest
Made sure I could
Breathe easily again
I was stunned that someone had
Saved me
For a while I was too scared
To even dip my toes back in
But you taught me how to swim again
How to stay afloat
Now when I'm in the water
I still dread the return of that grip on my ankles
But I hold true to the surface
And calmly drift away

The multifarious words
That left your lips
Were always oh so pretty
Like the ripest red and green
apples
You picked them
Meticulously from your tree
Each one tasting more
delicious
Than the last
As you spoke them, your
smile was
Almost sickly sweet

On your tongue danced
flowers,
Sweet roses
Whose petals caressed my
senses
Leaving me infatuated, dumb
And far too slow to notice
How sharp the thorns were
And that you had started to
cut me
While I was obsessed with the
promises
You'd fed me
Eating them all with an
unstoppable hunger
I'd willingly walked into the
trap
With my eyes wide open
But seeing nothing
Oblivious to your threat

When your mask slipped
away
Revealing what you really
were
No facade or pretty tricks
Could hide you anymore
My rose tinted glasses had
been
Snatched away

I finally saw the liar
That had played me for a fool
Like a cheap fiddle
Out of time
And full of cracks

Deep down in my battered
heart
A fire began to burn
It grew and grew
Until my body was nothing
but
A raging inferno
I let you think I was still
unaware
I let you think you had your
prize
But when you least expected
it
I spat red hot daggers directly
at your heart

I was underestimated
Undervalued
I will take your promises
I will rip them from my mind
Together with
Your vows of love and lust
And you can watch me if you
like
As I take a match to them all
And burn them into nothing
But an ash filled nightmare
Left behind to rot

You've always had an attitude
Some may say a misplaced faith
Your deluded sense of reality
Makes me want to use my fists
To beat my way out of this nightmare
Your incessant need to be right
Leaves a sour taste in the mouth
Of anybody you speak to
Grating
Like the sharp blades of a saw
Cutting into soft wood
You are a sophomaniac
Content to make others feel bad
Whilst you topple on the pedestal
You've placed yourself upon
And as you gallop around on your high horse
What is it that you're frightened of?
Is your fragile ego at risk?
Or are you worried that we will see
That beneath the mask
And the words you spit like shards of glass
Is somebody quite mundane?
Don't lay the blame
On all the rest
For your own miserable failings
Don't expect us to sit back
Accepting the twisted
Coping methods you've created
To make sure you feel okay and safe
Your insecurity should not be ours to bear
Indomitable, adamant, unrelenting, insistent
Intransigent, obdurate, unshakeable, dictatorial
Frustrating and pathetic
Kill them with kindness, they say
So to that, we say
In a world where you can be anything
Try not to be a cunt

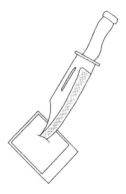

There is an intense longing
An unbridled desire that transforms itself
Into lustful thoughts and feelings of fire
Dangerous sins of the flesh

With an obsessive desire to feed ourselves
We overindulge until we're full
Gluttony to the point of waste
Ripping through the fruits of the earth

We pursue precious material
With a rapacious need to own it all
A greed to always have whatever we want
The sins of desire

Together we have a lack of feeling
The absence of love
We sloth and lay about without a care
For our failure to act when needed

Filled with an uncontrollable rage
We actively seek vengeance
Until everyone around us feels our wrath
And we are left alone, smouldering

We watch in disgust, at what we are not
Severed from each other
We are green with an envy
That is weighing down our souls

We are dangerously selfish
Weak minded with a strong bias
We are all filled with pride
The father of all sins

Somewhere deep inside
Locked away in
My blackened heart
Away from the summer days
Filled with funfairs
And white sandy beaches
You'll find it
Captive behind
A great iron gate
Sealed with a rusty padlock
To which only I hold the key;
A graveyard
Quiet and eerie
Full of everything and
Everyone
That has ever hurt me
A vast space
Full of anguish
Locked away entirely
Out of sight
Out of mind
That is except for the days
That I don't want to ride the carousel
Or feel the sand between my toes
Or the cool waves at my ankles
And instead I want to
Take the key
And unlock the gate
To visit the graves
Maybe take some flowers
Convinced that if perhaps I plant
The seeds between their bones
Eventually a garden will bloom
And I will no longer have to keep you all
Locked away
And I can start to enjoy my visits

Here we are again
Old friend
The little hand is on the three
And the big hand
On the twelve
And I can't help but greet you with
A knowing, loving smile
This is our finest hour
Basking in the peace and quiet
Of the middle of the night
Will always bring comfort
To people like us
Glass on glass
Makes a satisfying 'clink'
As I pour another whisky
To pass the time
The reflections
In the golden liquid catch my eye
As I reflect
On golden years gone by
How many times have we played this game?
There is a soft, familiar burn
As it passes down my throat
Oak and fire, warming me from within
Forever cherished companions
We sit together
During this lonely hour
The clock, the bottle and me
Passing the time
Just old friends, together
Until a new day begins to rise
And I smile and softly hum
Here comes the sun
Du du du du

There is a place,
I think I built myself,
Tucked just out of sight
Full of everything I've ever lost
Taken there to stew
Gather dust and wait
Until we need to call on them
I don't really remember
But I was convinced
Or at least pretty sure
I had placed you there
Upon the shelf
Between the jars
Of forgotten memories
Lids tightly shut
Not moving
Sat there in silence
In the dark
But now I'm starting to think
Perhaps it was you
That put me there
And I am the one
That was left to gather dust
I faintly remember your silhouette
As you walked out the door
And the last shard of light
Disappeared as it closed behind you
And now it's you
Who moves further and further away
From remembering where you left me

I remember you
How could I ever fucking forget?
My mother had warned me
About people like you
I always thought
That I'd remember her advice
But of course in the moment, I chose not to
Because she forgot to tell me
How exciting it could be
I remember how it started
Softly, with shyness
And secrets whispered to the wind
I remember the days
When we were a single entity
A bunch of tangled wires that would spark
And start a fire
If someone tried to straighten us out
Or organise our chaos
I remember the red-hot arguments
Where we spat daggers
That stabbed into our chests
Until one of them finally
Delivered the landing blow
We continued this way
For years
Trying to fight the odds
But undeniably something was between us
An invisible poison that we had both become addicted to
Yes, I remember you
But I don't remember love
When I do

There will always be a part of me
That cares
No matter how much time
Passes us by
And how much sand
Falls through the hourglass
I'll still be that figure
In the distance
Always quietly with the best of you
And though the rope
That used to be
Lassoed around our hearts
And our necks
Is now nothing more than
A single thread
Moments from snapping
And being gone forever
What will never be gone
Is me
2 o'clock in the morning
When my lips taste like rum
And I can't help but whisper a hello
Down the line
Hoping that wherever you are
You might stop
Listen
And reply

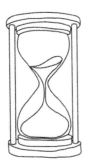

You are always fire and ice
Often your blood is boiling
So hot I can't bear to touch you
Out of fear of burning my own fingertips
The next thing you are freezing
So cold I still can't bear to touch you
Out of fear of the chill seeping into me
And leaving me with frostbite

You are always up and down
One day you're full of life and soaring
So magical and free
Every waking moment is a dream
When we're together
The next day you're on the floor, motionless
So quiet and distant
That every waking moment is a nightmare
And I'm left wishing we were apart

You are always sweet and sour
Often so loving and understanding
That it feels like we're thinking as one person
As every word you say is dripping with
The sweetest honey
Other days you're nothing but vicious
So violent and frightening
Your tongue has transformed into a viper
And every poisonous word stings

You are always split down the middle
Two halves of the same person
Each side battling for control
A tug of war I've found myself
Stuck refereeing
Praying that my favourite side wins today
And I can let my guard down again

I wish you were here
With that mischievous look in your eyes
Bags of craziness
Tucked under each arm
And that silly grin across your face
Ready to take my day from
Mundane to mad
Without even having to try
All you usually have to do
Is unscrew a bottle top
And offer me a sip

I wish you were here
With your obnoxiously loud laugh
Slamming your hand on a table
As you laugh at your own joke
Tears in your eyes
Chasing away all the peace and quiet
Causing people to turn their heads
To stop and stare
But you'd always stare right back
Laughing even louder
Not giving a single fuck
Because you were just having fun

I wish you were here
Annoying and distracting
Pulling my attention in a million different directions
Giving me a headache
And stomach cramps
From all the laughter
And the absolute silliness of it all
Always the life and soul
Always the joker

I really wish you were here

We were both stood
At the opposite ends of life
Paralysed by an invisible force
That kept our feet firmly in
One place
And it would be that way until
One day we noticed
That the other was there, waiting, looking on
And catching a glance was all it took
A burst of pure energy
Nothing we'd ever felt before
And suddenly
We were running
Towards each other
At the speed of light
Everything a blur
Like two atoms
Firing towards each other
Destined to smash together
And when we did
The Universe felt it
This tiny,
Microscopic moment
Where time stood still
And nothing else mattered
Proving there has always been magic
Buried within human contact
And once our skin had touched
Once our rib cages were forced together
And our hearts collided
We were joined together
And in that moment
Of molecules and atoms
All jostling for position
We had it all
Light,
Heat,
And Life
We are the Universe
And when it was over
We existed
In a perfectly stable state
Together

Love
Is without a doubt
The greatest burden of all
It changes us
Breaks us
And it can even kill
The best parts of us
But sometimes there are,
Secret smiles
Shared beneath bedsheets,
And inside jokes
Told over coffee
A feeling of safety
Just from being near
And soft, absentminded touches
That set your skin on fire
It is within these
Seemingly futile moments that perhaps
Love
Doesn't seem to be quite
The burden after all
Instead, a blessing
Tranquillity and contentment
It is a gift
Perhaps even,
The greatest gift of all
That we have all been burdened with

I fall in love with you
All over again
At 9:00 a.m.
When you are just waking up
Sleep filled eyes
And soft smiles
A sight I'm never tired of seeing

I fall in love with you
All over again
At 3:00 p.m.
As you rush around the house
Finding things to do
To fill the time
Always needing something
To keep your hands busy

I fall in love with you
All over again
At midnight
When you are sleeping peacefully
And the only thing I can hear
Is the sound of you breathing
As I quietly curl up
In the warmth radiating from you

I fall in love with you
Over and over again
Every single hour
Of every single day
All I ever need to do
Is open my eyes

My br ai n must have gLitc hEd
When I met you
A malfunction that
Temporarily lowered the defences
Around my heart
Allowing you access
With just enough time
To sneak in,
Steal it,
And claim it
For your own

With tentative pinkies
We each grip one end
Of the wishbone
Hoping and praying
We'll be the one to win
This friendly duel
Of good fortune
Both having more than enough things
To wish for
Both aware that other needs it just as much
But selfishly wishing
Only for our own success
We take a deep breath
Close our eyes
Countdown and
Pull as it snaps in half
Who will be brave enough to look first?

Loving you meant
Being forced again and again
To play your twisted games
And show my hand
With no chance in hell of
Ever winning
It is always dealer's choice with you
New rules made up on the spot
To put me at a constant disadvantage
Whenever I start to get a foothold
You'd change the game, again
Playing with a trick deck
And loaded dice
The stakes were always high
More than I could really afford
And as I played and played
I slipped further and further
Into your pocket
You would win
And I'd lose everything, every time
Facing you
Across the table
With your perfect poker face
Smirking behind
Mountains of chips
You'd gambled from right under my nose

Trapped inside a nightmare
Convinced you're not really gone
I can't accept it
Won't accept it
Realising I'll never see you smile again

My blood is boiling
I am filled with hatred for the world
And everything left in it
How could you do this?
How could you leave me?

Given the chance I'd do anything
For just one more day
One more drink, one more dance
I'm fucking begging you
Take me instead

Another empty bottle in your name
Another lonely, sleepless night
Wondering if this will ever end
How long can I keep this up?
I never feel whole anymore

Now I see you in the sunsets of summer
I see you in the snowy scenes of winter
And I know while you're not here,
You've never really left
Always by my side

You told me all along
One day you'd break my heart
I never thought it would be like this
But now I welcome the pain
If it means I got the chance to know you

When the grief comes
And my goodness, it comes
It is easy to sit
In the sadness
Building up walls to hide behind and
Dwelling on the past
Things that might have been
Things that could have been different
Things that should have been said
All going round and round in your head
Stuck in a loop you can't seem to break
But when you're ready
When the walls come down
You should try to remember
The good times
The things that were
The things you wouldn't change
The things you did say
And toast them
While it's the harder path to walk
It will always be the most rewarding
Because at the end is a library
With no late return fees
Full of memories
Today I chose to remember your laugh
And on top of that,
All the laughs we shared together
Tomorrow I might choose to remember your warmth
Or how you used to sing
I will choose to remember your best bits
And your worst
I will still miss you, every day
And while my heart will sometimes still ache
With the sadness of knowing you're not here
I owe it to you
To keep pushing on
With our memories
Stored safely on the shelves in my library

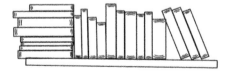

There was a time when all I
knew
Was the constant slog
Mundanity
Everything the same
Day in
Day out
Just shades of grey
Not even 50 of them
Painting everything
A shitty shade of plain
Everything was quiet
And I was asleep

When in a sudden explosion
Of colour and noise
You came along
Crashing right into me
Overwhelming my senses
with new
Tastes and smells and sights
You turned my world
completely on its head
And left me reeling

Stuck in a constant state of
confusion
I tried to make
Heads or tails of who you
were
And what you'd done to me
Stuck inside a fever dream
Where nothing made sense
any more
My skin was always tingling
My chest was always tight
Colours had turned from dull
to vibrant
Suddenly there was sound
And everything was different
Better
Almost overnight
It was complete and utter
madness

And that I had been craving it
The madness
All along
And that I would take the
crazy dreams and
The breathlessness
If it meant that you stayed
around a while
And showed me what it was
To feel alive

Love Is:
Asking someone to let you know that they got home safely
Waking up earlier just to make them breakfast
Reminding somebody to wear sunscreen when it's hot (and even when it's not)
Running after the ice cream van together at 30 odd years old
Being able to sit comfortably together in silence, simply existing
Watching the same old shit on tv and still laughing

Love is everywhere
In the big, grand gestures
And the small, mundane moments
Keeping us safe and sound
Reminding us exactly why it is good
That we're here

One day,
When I'm gone
And you find yourself
Wanting to reminisce
Remember me as a time of day
More specifically as
Twilight
Tucked safely in between
Daylight and darkness
That is where our memories lay
Comforting like a soft, warm blanket
Or as sharp and cutting as a fine blade
Use them
As a defence mechanism
As personal therapy
They'll always be slightly out of reach
But still, they will wait for you
Should you ever slow down at the right time
To need them

What matters most
Is that we tried
I mean,
We really gave it our all
Walked through every fire
And burnt our feet
Over and over again
With fractured minds
And broken hearts

Together, we bled

When you're nothing but broken pieces on the floor - it's up to you to put yourself back together again.

Therapy

To open up is tough. It was one of the hardest things I've ever done

It took me too long
It's not just letting the words leave your mouth
It's seeing the eyes of the person you're talking to
The response they give
To let the tide of regret burst through the dam
That you've built in your mind
Flood your brain
Try not to drown
Things should never be the same now, hopefully
Things might even be better

But at least the pressure is released
Chin up and keep moving forward kiddo

Another hazy morning
My bad choices littered everywhere
Amongst the mess, destruction
And chaos that you left behind
The empty bottles smash
As I throw them in the bin
Fragile, sharp and dangerous
Just like the promises you made me
Last night's attempt to forget
Turn into all I can think about today
In a desperate attempt
To escape
I just go round and round
And come full circle
Back to the start
Or is it the end?
Whatever this place is
It just resembles you
The only thing residing
Inside my mind now
This needs to be the last time
It all needs to go
Everything
Boxes full of memories
Bags full of clothes
All thrown together in a pile
Wreckage tainted with despair
This choice needs to be final
With one last look I light the match
And finally set it on fire

Life is full of
Decisions to be made
And I am no stranger to
Making questionable,
Occasionally bad,
Choices
Sometimes even on purpose
But that's the thing about
Being alive
You always get a choice
Yes or no
Up or down
Forwards or backwards
Black or white
It's all completely up to you
Terrifying, right?
One wrong move and you're spiralling
But a right one can send you soaring like a rocket
If only you're brave enough to make that choice
To completely succumb to it all
Send yourself full steam ahead
Charging bravely
Into the battlefield
We call life
For better or worse
And now here I am once again
Stuck in a moment of choice
Stood completely still
The chaos of the battle
All around me
In slow motion
Facing a crossroads
Trying to desperately figure out which way to go
To be brave
And choose
Hoping to propel myself that bit farther
Towards my nirvana

I've caged myself
And focused hard on creating a beast
That can all at once
Protect me and
Empower me
A raging bull
Determined to tear the world apart
Leaving behind nothing
But a trail of destruction
Just to prove that
I wasn't weak
Screaming voices
Laced with anger
Are all I can ever hear
The dissonance never stops
Alarms ring constantly
Everywhere I go
Eventually I will burn out
Leaving nothing but a pile of ashes
And deep regrets
But I won't listen to the warnings
And it will take me too long
To realise, finally
That the danger they were alerting me to
Was me all along

Waking up in a nylon hell
Another night of pushing the boundaries
Too far
Pins and needles riddle my brain
I'm still floating on the dark side of the moon
The lightning was ridden
And the damage was done
Body broken
Brain mush
Senses dulled
My eyes and brain flirt
Flickering
Deciding what is real
Through the haze comes a guardian angel
Suffering from her own self induced
Morning after the night before
We journeyed together through the magic forest
Healing and connecting
We emerged from the other side complete
And whole
Once more
Ready for battle again that very night
What better way to learn
That we are only human

There is a lot of beauty
In ordinary things
Like friendship

Outside
The early morning sun
Was causing my nylon coffin to become
Suffocating
The morning after the night before
Left me struggling to piece together
What on earth had happened this time
As I struggled to shake off the fog
That was making it impossible to think straight
I realised I was not alone
Beside me stood a stranger
Dealing with the repercussions of his own
Bad choices
Together we tackled it head on
Keeping each other sane
Taking a bad situation and crafting it
Into a newfound friendship
Laced with vulnerability
And gratitude
Happy to have found each other
In the exact moment that we both needed
A helping hand

There is something magical
About kindness
When it finds you unexpectedly

Inside,
The entire world
Separated from each other for the first time
Stuck, stop-starting
Finding new ways
To keep ever growing fears and boredom
At bay
Forced to wait, to stick it out
Not knowing what will come next
In solidarity
Battling an invisible, mutual enemy

Outside
Nature is healing
In the quiet of our slowed down lives
Mother nature, smiling
Mother nature, laughing
Mother nature, breathing freely again
Splashing in clearer waters,
Dancing in cleaner air,
Earth lives on
Waiting for our return
Hoping that we will have learned valuable lessons

Inside
Together we can take time
To talk
To catch up with friends we've been
Too busy to see
To laugh with loved ones stuck in their own homes
To read, to sing, to dance, to bake fucking banana bread,
To breathe
Or do absolutely sweet nothing
Together alone
We wait patiently
Until we can go outside again

Drink in hand
Powering on
Determined not to submit
This time
Quietly watching the world wake up around us
Above our heads, clouds swirl
Like fresh candy floss
Painting the sky in such a way you'd think
Michelangelo himself had been holding the brush
Dawn,
For the early risers
And late nighters
Content to stumble,
We mumble,
"Good morning"
Raise our glass
To a world that failed us
Try as we might
To make things right
We always seem to end up at the bottom

The faces and the places
They've all changed
Either tired and old
Or shiny and new
Completely different from what I
Remember
And yet somehow
Exactly the same
Still grey
Still dingy
Still angry
Still ugly
Just with a slap of fresh paint
Here and there
Trying to disguise itself into something
Fresh and new
Maybe next time I come back
I won't recognise you
Maybe you won't recognise me, either
With a bit of luck

Although rare, these days
There is something so extraordinarily special
About dancing
Until the early morning hours
With friends you see too little of
Because life gets in the way
But when these moments come it's as if
They were never gone
All of a sudden you're laughing
With no idea what started you off
And all you know is that
Your stomach can't possibly hurt
More than it does in this moment of
Chaotic bliss
So you welcome the pain and
The tears streaming down your face
And you catch yourself
Contemplating
How much you love these misfits
For just being themselves
For always being there
Through it all
Something real to cling onto
In a world as ridiculous as this
So you hug them tightly
And you keep dancing
Like nobody is looking
Like you don't give a fuck that
Normality is hiding just around the corner
Waiting to jump on you the second it can
As the moon shines on brightly

A narrow path
Leads to a row of unique,
But simple buildings
Cows moo a welcome to me
As they graze happily
Only feet away
Excitement grows as I
approach
My haven
The gate creaks quietly as I
open it
I exhale and smile
As my head empties itself,
finally
Instant relief
Breathe easy
Relax

The water from the river
flows gently
On it boats pass me by
Steered by friendly strangers
Waving
Feeling the same relief as I do
A dog in a life jacket stands
tall on a hull
Captain of the waterways

Inside the simple, little house
All life's complications seem
to melt away
Open a bottle of wine
Take a seat
Read a book
Catch a fish
Get the bbq going
Filling the air with the
promise of dinner
And more wine

The view here is serene
A picturesque place
Plucked directly from a
Claude Monet painting

And placed all around me
Good food feeds the body
Great company feeds the soul
I relish in the abundance

As the sun starts to set
The water becomes a mirror
Reflecting hues of
Yellow, orange and red
Until the sun disappears
Down the middle of the river
And glorious purples fill the
sky

Perfection
Such a simple, special place
Never change

Tomorrow is a mystery
As it should be
An entirely blank canvas
Ready and waiting
For us
To open our eyes and
Splash our paint all over it
To make it anything and
Everything
We want it to be

Tomorrow has no expectations
It holds no limitations
Makes no assumptions
Casts no judgement
On you, or whatever you plan to do with it
It is a fresh start
A chance to try it all again
To make it better than before
A promise and sense of hopefulness
That no bad day can take away

Yes, tomorrow
Is a mystery
Waiting to be greeted with open arms
And a patient smile
Wrapping itself around you
As you ready yourself for another day of
What ifs and maybes
So you brush your teeth
Comb your hair
Clench your fists
And get ready to give it hell

"Shall I compare thee to
a summer's day?"
No, never
Thank you very much
Unless the day you have in mind
Is the one that begins
With a subtle calmness
Before transcending
With blurred edges and pastel skies
Filling your eyes and luring you into
A false sense of security
Then quicker than you can blink
The serenity
Turns completely on its head
Gone without a trace
A storm comes rumbling in
Raging like a bull
Shattering the illusion
As clear skies turn to grey
Catching you off guard
Forcing you to either take cover
And hide until it's all blown over
Or tackle it head on
Risking being blown away
By the sheer ferociousness
Of an untethered rage
Mixed with a hint of sass
Gone as quickly as it came
A whirlwind of
Chaos and spontaneity
That's the kind of summers day I'll always be
Entirely unpredictable
The perfect storm

When I'm looking
For something dangerous
To feed my soul
To soothe it and to
Settle it down
I need to hear that
Familiar sound
Of the cork popping
Food isn't the
Nourishment I need
Some days I want to
Pick up a bottle
Of something that will
Burn my throat
And set my soul on fire
Get me into a little trouble
And then grab
A pen
That I can stab directly
Into my heart
And let the blood turn into
Ink that I can use
To my advantage
Pop on some Elton John
Hercules himself
Letting his voice bring out the best
In me
A sound that can crawl
Beneath my skin
And get stuck within
All the nooks and crannies
Deep inside
That I can't let anybody see
But will never be hidden
Most of the time
My soul is hungry
Starved, even
Craving something magical
That will allow it to explode
And shatter everything around it

Gentle sprinkles
Rain down from a bleak, grey sky
Floating slowly into the softest landing
Covering the world in a light dusting of magic
Turning even the most
Drab landscapes
Into a masterpiece
Each step crunches underfoot
As I take a walk through
The vast white and find a place
Entirely untouched
Running my hand across the snow
It is almost too soft to feel
Were it not for the cold that blasts through my fingers
As I roll it into balls with childlike glee
And throw them
Leaving marks on walls and trees
And friends
Together we stop and build
A snowman
Who has a carrot for a nose
Absentmindedly I run my finger
Across a coated windscreen
To draw something childish
And giddily run away
Skipping into the winter bliss
Before returning home
To sit by the fire
And warm my feet
Sipping on whisky
Whilst it continues to fall outside
Wrapping a thick white blanket
Around everything
As far as the eye can see

And just like that
It was over
After fighting for so long
To keep my head
Above the surface
But below the clouds
I eventually hit
A wall
Exhausted and weak I lay there
Wondering if this was it now
The fire inside me had burnt out
And I had started to choke
On the smoke left behind
My fingers were coated in thick ash
So that everything I touched was smeared
In black streaks
And all I could do was sit and wonder
Where the heat had gone
I felt something stir
Like a rumble in my stomach
As something started to rise
From the ashes
And I realised that all it would take
Was a spark
The smallest flash
To bring back the flames
So I began to work
I clawed my way back to my feet
From the floor I'd been stranded on
Until I could move again
And with every step
The flame grew bigger
Stronger
Hotter
Until I was nothing more than a
Raging inferno
Ready to burn anything that tried to
Smother me again

Time is an entirely
Abstract concept
Sitting here now
At a cluttered desk
Covered with lists of things
I have convinced myself
I want to do
Or need to do
But can never seem to find the time
To do
On the shelf above me
I can hear the clock
Ticking every second away
Counting down to the next whatever
Counting down to the inevitable end
Of our existence on this planet
I am very used to saying
I just don't have enough time
With a schedule full of things to do,
Places to be,
People to see
The human construct
That rules our lives
That we somehow have too much of
And at the same time not enough
Because some always manages to slip away
It's a trap
I'd do anything to escape
To untangle myself
From the grip of time
And the endless road
That seems to stretch out
Forever in front of me
It's so heavy
And exhausting
But exciting
And terrifyingly uncontrollable
And it does nothing but haunt me

I long for summer days
Where the brightness of the sun
Hurts my eyes
And everybody has the smell of sun cream
Coming from the warmth of their flushed skin
People sizzling on the common
Sausages sizzling on the bbq
And me
Sat cross legged on blankets
With all my friends
Mood boosting music providing the soundtrack of our summer
And nothing but good times
Are being had
Hands slightly sticky
From holding an ice cream and
Desperately trying to finish it
Before it melts all over our knees
And we become a target
For the wasps and the bees
Bring me the long days I'm dreaming of
I want them now
I don't even mind getting up early
Because 6am is a lot more appealing
When a blue sky is waiting
Just outside the door
I can't wait for
Seaside swims and
Pub garden laughs
Dinners outside and
Cool evening showers
Hopefully not alone
I can't wait to fill every day with as much fun
As I can manage
So Summer, if you're listening
Don't make me wait too much longer
My mouth is already watering at the thought
Of that sweet, salted caramel ice cream

Good people
Go to heaven
But the bad ones
Make their dinner on a mirror
Grab a neat spirit
Turn the fucking volume up
And listen to something real,
Raw and powerful
Always returning to the gods
That make it timeless
Like Freddie
Strutting his stuff in yellow and white
Or Elton
In his star-studded glasses and sequins
Or Bowie
Sparkling like a star man in the sky
Guy-Manuel and Thomas
Robots rocking and getting lucky
Billie-Joe, Mike and Tre
American idiots at their fucking finest
Gerard, Frank, Mikey and Ray
Riding a float in the Black Parade
Or Jamiroquai
With JK's hats and plenty of canned heat
Our hearts are kick-started by the Mötley Crüe
And Mick's thunderous guitar riffs
So here's to us
Flicking through the vinyl
Smelling the history
Picking the one that speaks to us
The most
Feel free to down your drink
And join me
As I let fucking loose

I have a much softer tone set
On the alarm clock
These days
To try and wake me gently
From my sleep
But it's still an all too familiar disturbance
That I would rather not be hearing
As I'm pulled from my dream
Into another new day
It's brighter this time of year
And although my old body
Stretches and rises easier
Than it does in the colder months
It is still somewhat of a struggle
The birds sing
As I begin my morning rituals
Providing the perfect soundtrack
Whilst I stand in the garden
And take in some fresh air
Reflecting calmly
For just a few moments before
Hot coffee and toast
Get my engines roaring
The steam and aroma filling the air
As I hold the mug underneath my face
Breathing in through the nose
And out through the mouth
Just like I've been taught to do
As my daily dose of courage
That comes in prescription form
Settles in and
Gets to work
Helping me through another day
With a calmer mind
And a smile

I can't fucking wait
After a year inside
Finally some hope
That's all anyone has wanted, right?
The return of normality
And the promise that soon, we will be free
To sing and dance
Together again

I need to feel it
That thumping
And throbbing
That fills your senses
As you're walking towards
Endless stages
Of geniuses at work
Surrounded by friends
And strangers
In stranger conditions
Beneath a bright blue
Summer sky

It gets louder still, until
The thumps and throbs begin to morph together
With the quiet hum of music
As mids and highs begin
To take over
Sucking you in
Pulling you forward to the good times ahead
Not too far in the distance
Teasing and enticing you
Forcing your best foot forward
In desperation of the rush that comes
When the sun goes down
And the lights turn up
And for a split second the crowd is
Silent
Before erupting into
A deafening cheer
And you're in the happiest place
You could be
And best of all
We're free

We don't write for
The fun of it
Or even for the thrill
There are no such things
When your head is filled with white noise
And words that rattle
With every step you take

We write to take the pressure
Off our aching shoulders
And sore backs
To lessen the overbearing weight
Of the thoughts and feelings
Weighing us down
That make functioning normally
Almost impossible

We write to clean out the words
That are trapped between
Our teeth
And stuck on the tip of our tongue
That we can't bring ourselves to say
Out loud
So we scribble them in messy penmanship
Instead

We write to cut our heavy hearts open
At 3am when we're liquored up
And our vessels are bursting
Dripping ink instead of blood
Across the pages
As we stitch ourselves back together again
With every letter written

We write to survive
We write to live

It is easy
To lose yourself
Down a deep, dark hole
Of self-pity
Going deeper and deeper until
You forget how to lift
Your head from the pillow in the morning

It is easy
To push away any offers of help
To dismiss people's worried comments
To choke out a daily 'I'm fine'
Rather than admit to yourself
And everybody else
That you don't remember what fine feels like

It is easy
To give up
But it's much harder to fight
Grit your teeth
Raise your head
Clench your fists
And just admit
That you are drowning
And that you need to cling to your friends
Until a sliver of hope
Begins to nestle inside of you
And maybe you can start to live again

You take aim
Over and over again
Squeeze the trigger
And fire
A sudden spark
And a loud bang
But I don't so much as flinch
As the bullet comes flying towards me
Piercing the air before
Hitting me dead on target
But it just bounces off
Landing on the ground
Smoking, spent and pathetic
Surrounded by all the others
All the hollow point lies
You've desperately tried
To shoot me with before
When will you learn that
I am bulletproof
And you cannot hurt me now
Neither your full metal madness
Or your fifty-calibre chaos
Can penetrate the armour
I have welded to my skin
I will take anything you throw at me
I'll stand firm
On a mountain of gold casings
Until you empty your last clip
And finally lay down your weapons
Surrendering, defeated.

We all grow up thinking that
Somehow
We can change the world
And deep down, we want to
Leave our mark
To do something truly awesome
But in reality
Not many of us are actually insane enough
To get it done
Maybe I haven't changed the world yet
Probably never will, either
But I've done some cool shit in my time
And I've paid attention to those
Who never clapped for me
That put me down
And told me no
And laughed
Behind my back
As I tried to push forward
Whilst they were stood still doing nothing
I took my thumbs off the PlayStation controller
My eyes off the television set
And with my feet firmly planted
I put my pen to paper
Creating something from nothing
People say it takes 100 years
For a plastic bag to break down
Well, I can do that at the drop of a hat sweetie
Which I think is pretty fucking impressive, don't you?
So don't try and interrupt me
Whilst I'm busy
Doing exactly what you told me
I could never do
So take this
And walk

We artists know
That there is no woman better,
No woman more
Attentive,
And trustworthy
Than the moon.
She keeps our secrets
She listens to them all
And never passes judgement

She has a special place
For the biggest secrets
Trapped inside tears
As they fall on soft pillows
From puffy, red eyes
And flushed, pink cheeks
She holds on tight
To the most truthful ones
She giggles and appreciates
The ones that tumble and fall
Slurred and broken
From drunken lips

But the ones she hides the deepest
Are the ones that are whispered
Almost too softly to hear
By the broken hearts
That are trying their hardest
To mend themselves
Before the obnoxious sun comes up
And he shines his light on our business
Exposing it for everyone to see

Desperate to learn something new
We artists know
That there is no fucker worse
Than him
That giant, yellow gossip

The great Billy Connolly
Once said
"Listen to the comedians
And poets
They're telling the truth"
He's right, you know
Our pens are always connected
Directly to our hearts
Whether they're in our chests
Or on our sleeves
We let ourselves
Bleed freely
For everyone to witness
Maybe you think that makes us brave
Maybe you think that makes us foolish
But you should just know that we're
Desperately trying
To pull ourselves from the wreckage
And our words are the only weapon we have
To keep fighting
So we'll keep performing
And pouring
And perfecting
So that you can keep listening to
And watching
The comedians
And the poets

This one is for the
Creative types
The artists
The writers
The actors
The comics
The ones who were told
Constantly
That their dreams would
amount
To nothing more
Than a hobby
Hidden behind closed doors
To be dusted off as a cure to
Boredom
Or to show your kids one day
Well
Here's to us
Cheers
Raise a glass
To the misfits
Whether you think you're
talented
Or not
Struggling, but enjoying
Every moment
Because we found something
That sets our souls on fire
And equally
Does our fucking head in
We get to create
New worlds
That we can fall into
New songs to sing
New jokes to laugh at
New images to see
New things to imagine
And people to offend
With our unwavering
commitment
To it all
So keep on creating, gang
Because no matter what they
say

The world will always need
Our hustle
Even if does amount to
nothing more
Than our favourite hobby
Or our favourite excuse to
drink

I sign cards with a kiss in the loop of the g of my name because that's what my mum and nan do

I don't like to shut doors in my house because growing up my mum never did

Sometimes, as a treat, I like to eat poppadom's before a curry because that's the way round my grandparents would eat it

I cross my legs when a train passes because my nan taught us it was bad luck if we didn't

I like to have lime cordial with vodka because that's how my best friend likes it

I always have my baths far too hot because that's how my mum takes them

I like to wear my hair in a high bun when my fringe is sitting nicely because one time my brother said it suited me and I never forgot how that made me feel

If I get a stain on my clothes, I wash them and put them on the grass because that's how my nan taught me to get them out

The first time I listen to an album I listen to it the entire way through in order because my sister told me that's how it was supposed to be heard

I like to have a banana milkshake at the end of a night out because that's what my mum does, and she swears it helps the hangover

I always wear hair grips curved side down because a co-worker told me once they stay in better that way

I always try to say happy birthday at midnight or as soon as I wake up because that's what my childhood best friend would do for me

I take photos of every pretty sunrise or sunset because my nan always does

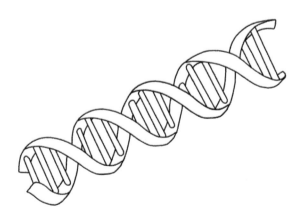

When I do the washing up I always leave it to dry on a tea towel
because that's what nan did
I prefer my coffee from a cafetière because that's how Chloë makes
it
I love bacon and egg rolls for breakfast because that's what mum
always makes
I keep cash in different places because dad said that was sensible
And I would give anybody the shirt off my back, because that's what
he always does for me.
I drink my whisky neat because grandad said "that's how it's done
kid"
On birthdays we always play Happy Birthday to Ya by Stevie
Wonder because that's tradition
If I smoke a cigarette I always twist the last of the tobacco out of the
butt because I saw a girl in Bolivia do it once
I leave my clothes on the floor because it drives my mum crazy
And I never make my bed because an old flame told me it makes
them more comfortable
I like my music on vinyl because my music teacher told me that's
how it sounds the best
I wear a lot of black because my Belgian friends told me it was cool
I always wait by the phone at 10:10am on my birthday because my
parents will always call me on the dot of the time I was born
I always take a beer to a sunset or a summit because countless
travellers I met all did the same
I always try to do my best and put others first because that's what
was ingrained in me.

We are all made up of odds and ends
Collected from everybody we've ever met
Unique but connected
And I will always think that
That is beautiful

The lid had been sealed
Airtight
For what felt like forever
It took all my remaining strength
To grip it
To twist and pull
Until it started to budge
With teeth gritted and muscles shaking
I held on until it opened
Just a crack
That was all it needed
I was helpless to the force
Of the words that exploded out
Shattering the glass into
Razor sharp shards of truth
Cutting and slicing everything in sight
As they travelled away
Too fast to be heard
Laced with desperation
Venom
And a sprinkle of hope
Never to be shut away again
All that remained
Was a puff of smoke hanging in the air
And pieces glass
Reflecting in the sun
As far as the eye could see

Are you:

Lonely
Oppressed
Standing still
Trembling

Now is the time to
Break free

When you're ready to return to the world - do it with your head held high and don't bother looking back.

Recovery

So
Here we go
Finally setting off
No, in fact I'm well and truly
Fucking off
This time I'm not looking for you
I've already done that
So many times
And look where it's got me
No, this time I'm looking for myself
Or at the very least
A nice Long Island Iced Tea
Somewhere hot
And exotic
Where even ordinary people
Seem to glisten in the sun
All that's left for me to do
Is work out how I'm going to get there
What combination of planes, trains
And automobiles
Will get me to an unknown destination
Dreaming of steel drums
Comfortable hammocks
And soft, sandy beaches
Surrounded by magnificent palm trees
With a cocktail in hand
And a clear head
Taking the time to find
What's missing

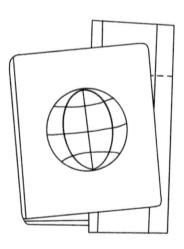

I sit back and relax
Pressing myself into the chair
Leaving all control packed
away
With the rest of my things
I am merely a passenger, now
Here for the ride
Nothing more
No expectations
No decisions to be made
The only feelings here are
Excitement and
Exhilaration
As the engine rumbles and
Roars to life
Before we speed down the
runway
Straight as an arrow

My eyes widen as
The whole machine leans
back
Our lives out of our own
hands
And placed firmly in the
hands of the pilot
The wheels leave the ground
And my stomach drops
As we climb and climb
Higher and higher
With every passing second

I rest my head next to the
windowpane
And put my hand on the glass
As it begins to frost over
Watching as the safety net
Of having both feet on the
ground
Is pulled from beneath me
And I am filled with a
nervous glee
Pumped full of adrenaline

We penetrate the clouds
Like a bullet
Bursting out the other side
Into the sudden calmness of
Nothing but sky
The sun is bright and blinding
The clouds are white wisps of
magic
Guiding us to a better place

I sit back
Pressing myself into my chair
I have no control over any of
this
And I love it.

Bukowski would write:
"How in the hell could a man
enjoy
Being awakened at 6:30 a.m.
by an
Alarm clock"
I feel that, man
Staggering through the dark
For nothing more than
The privilege of making
A rich person, richer
Expected to be grateful for
the opportunity
Just to make my ends meet
They watch over me
With their rules wrapped
around me like shackles
Don't forget, you can't take
Too many days off
And don't you dare think
About getting sick
Your life depends on it
It's pretty shitty
That hazy morning vision
Crazy hair,
Bags under my eyes
Heavy enough to drag me
down
Attempts to counter with
caffeine
Seem futile and pointless
The stranger in the mirror
Looks weak
A slave to somebody else's
machine
Plugged in
Pretending to enjoy
That quick breakfast
Forced down while watching
the clock
Brush my teeth
Comb my hair
Just to get ahead
Of the other sheep

In the motorway herd
Not today
No, today my hair can stay
wild
I'll make whatever I want for
breakfast
Whenever I feel like eating
Flick my slippers across the
room
Feet up
TV on
Close the curtains
Open some wine and
Drink it from the bottle
Flip out my notepad
Write this poem
And take back what's mine
While I can
Even if it's just for today

"Drink from the well
of yourself
and begin
again."
Hank said,
Ok then, I will

The close of a day
Activates the time machine
Behind my eyes
Even as I fall asleep
My brain remains so active
Transporting me somewhere
else entirely
As the machine whirls
Into action
Blasting me off into
Lucid visions
Of adventures in space
And canoeing down
A river
To an unknown destination
No longer the driver
But the passenger, instead
Happily being whisked away
Until suddenly I am
Flying in the sky
Like an eagle
Running through the trees
Forever more
Or
At least until the morning

Like a wolf
I see myself
Through the eyes of another
As a king
As a queen
Living in a castle
Surrounded by subjects
A soldier
On the frontier
An Astronaut
On the edge of the galaxy
All the things
I want to be suddenly
Entirely possible
In a world
Where I can't be hurt
But flourish instead
Limited only
By my own imagination
Blue Skies and
Happy thoughts

Happiness
You fickle fuck
Always a mysterious creature
A constant companion for some
If you can believe that
A stranger in the shadows for others
That's usually the truth
I've always known you
As elusive
Distant
Never quite able
To make up your mind
About whether you're staying or not
So, if I do know anything about you
It's that you're usually not one
To stick around
But lately something's different
I feel you around me
Almost constantly
Finally, I think, I find you in my company
Or am I perhaps in yours?
It doesn't matter
Because with a content sigh I say
Welcome
It doesn't matter the arrival was late
It's just good you're finally here
Let's hope you hang around
For a while

This morning I watched in
awe
As the sunlight hit a
spiderweb
At the perfect angle
A light breeze in the air
Came along to join it
Causing the web to shimmer
Right in front of my eyes
And I was completely
mesmerised
Watching it dance
And glisten
As if it was something
Entirely otherworldly

This afternoon as the sun
began
To go to sleep
The final rays
Found their way to my
window
Stretching out
And searching until they
found
The ring my mother left me
And thrust a rainbow against
The wall
Causing colours so vibrant
They remind me of her
Beautiful and radiant

The perfect homage

This evening I caught sight
Of the new, full moon
I watched as it
Settled in and waved
goodnight
To the sun
Its soft glow gently settling
In a puddle that had been left
By a nearby blocked drain
That was now working
overtime
As a mirror
Isn't it funny how something
that's usually so ugly
Can become something so
beautiful
If given a chance

Today the world has
reminded me
That beauty can be found in
everything
The mundane
The boring
Even the inconveniences
If only you take the time
To open your eyes
And see it

I am here to help
To give you the air you need
To breathe
And to take away the poison
Made by machines
That blankets the sky
I am colourful
I am scented
I am everything that awakens your
Senses
When the lights go out I go limp
Longing for the sun to rise
And I can come alive again
Dancing a dance with
The sunrise and
The sunset
I am always watching
Always listening
Always present
And all that I need from you
Is some water
And a nice spot in the sun
And I'll be your companion
For as long as you need me

Here's to the friends
Who have seen it all
And have stuck around to wait
And see what happens next
The ones that have spent countless nights
Dancing with you
On rooftops and tabletops
Big, stupid smiles on their faces
Welcoming the comedown they'll have to face
The next day
Because my god, wasn't it worth it?
Here's to the ones that noticed when
You started to dance slower and slower
Until you stopped dancing altogether
The ones that hugged you as you began to fall apart
So tightly that the pieces of your broken soul
Were forced to stay together
When they could have so easily shattered on the floor
Here's to them
For their patience
For their friendship
For their strength
For being the first ones to turn the music back on
Rock and roll, usually
And for putting a drink in your hand
The second you're back on your feet
And before you know it
That spark has returned
And you remember how to move your feet

Here I am
Almost at the end
With the finish line in sight
Exhausted and
Covered in scars
From walking through fire and glass
And weathering many storms
They serve as a stark reminder
Of everything I've battled
But
Whenever I get too close
To the finish line
I hit an obstacle and fall
Watching from the floor
As it suddenly gets up and moves
Another 100 yards away
Always just slightly out of reach
Leaving me face down on the tarmac
And I can't help but believe
That it's impossible
To ever cross the fucking thing
Stuck in an endless chase
Of glass, fire, storms, hope and disappointment
Before starting all over again

But perhaps
The destination isn't so important
Maybe it's the journey instead
And if I slowed down a little
I'd have time to focus on the obstacles
And maybe I could dodge a few next time
All of a sudden I'm not so desperate
To reach the end
But content
To take in my surroundings a little more
To step over the glass
And walk around the fire
Stay inside and let the storms pass
And write down all the stories I have
About trying to find my way
To that ever-absent finishing line
Because really, what's the rush?

I am grateful for the friendships
That I've found and lost
In people from all over the world
That manage to bring out the best
And sometimes the worst
In me

I am grateful for the family
That taught me
Who I am and
Where I come from
Before letting me loose to
Figure out the rest for myself
But always keeping a refuge for me
To come home to, when I need it

I am grateful for my body
For getting me through all the
Highs and lows
The late night parties
And the early morning regrets
For carrying me through
And allowing me to do it all again
Even if it does put up a bit more of a fight
Nowadays

I am grateful for this life
That taught me how to get back up
And try again
Full of adventures
And adventurers
That keep my heart full
And my soul on fire
Filling every day
With something to be
Grateful for

Another wave crashes onto the shore
Underneath a moonlit sky
Another adventure taking a toll
On my old legs
Another sun-soaked paradise for me to capture
With my lens
Another great mystery left unsolved
In ruins
Another group of new friends
Added to my contacts list
Another set of empty bottles
Littering the floor
Another half-read novel
Traded for something new
Another hungover morning
Spent planning our next move
Another flight booked on the credit card
I can't afford to pay off
Another month passing by
On the calendar
Another entry in the journal
To look back on later

Another day in the world
Simply living

It is strange
To look back on everything
Isn't it?
All the mountains you have
Painstakingly climbed
The crossroads you have
Successfully navigated
The deep holes you have
Tirelessly climbed back out of
Every rock bottom you've crawled away from
And to accept that, finally
You are happy
Or, at the very least
You're happy *enough*
Maybe even a little wiser too
If you were paying attention

Sometimes you can only sit and laugh
To yourself
Perched on the corner of a table
Swilling your drink
Slightly mesmerised by the liquid
As it swirls inside the glass
Catching the light
And showing off as the muted brown
Transforms into liquid gold
Knowing that nobody else here
Really, truly
Gets it
And that brings a little smile to your face
Sometimes it's better this way
Sometimes the stories you keep for yourself
Mean the most to you...

Like that time I played golf alone at night

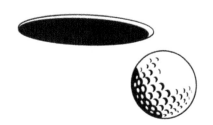

Remember when
You said we would never be good enough
We would always be a waste of space
Buncha low life good for nothins
Too interested in searching for the next high
Followed by the fear and the loathing
Of the low times
To ever amount to anything
But look at us now, baby
Not top of the food chain
But distinctly fucking average
Above average, occasionally
Which is good enough for us
When we're focused
Working tirelessly towards our dreams
Fuelled by the determination
To stick our fingers up at you
Even if it's only the once
So
Step aside and watch how it's done
How we don't shy away from hard work
And still manage to have more than our fair share
Of high times

The first, fresh flowers are
Bursting from the ground
In a much-needed explosion
Of vibrant colour
Spy them opening and showing off
With a confidence that comes only with
The beauty that they hold

The bees are buzzing
Just happy to have a place to work and play
The birds are singing
Earlier and earlier each morning
The trees are almost entirely green again
The sky is almost entirely blue
And the big yellow sun
Overseas it all
Brightening up our lives
As it stays around a little longer each day

People enjoy the cool grass
Between their toes
And the purple dye of an afternoon of
Blackberry picking
Between their fingers
Whilst the promise of warmth
And drinks by the cold sea
Float around their brains

Spring has finally arrived
And awoken something around us
I'm sure you can feel it, too

It's true that there is strength
In numbers
And there is no exception
When we are together
Our group holds a power
That makes us feel
Untouchable
We can't be stopped
Once we get started
We catch people watching us in awe
Out of the corner of their eyes
As we walk the walk
And talk the talk
Shoot shit
And sink shots
With nothing but
Confidence and
Charisma
Oozing from each and
Every one of us
We're the T-birds,
The Pink Ladies and even
The Reservoir Dogs
All rolled into one package
Effortlessly cool
On Saturdays
Cigarettes and whisky
Leather and wayfarers
Even the Warriors and the Scorpions
Would fear us
Whilst we're having nothing but fun
They wouldn't come out to play
Not when we're in town

What's more punk rock
Than living loud and fucking proud
Sticking a middle finger up
To all those who tried to knock you down

What's more punk rock
Than being nothing other than
Entirely authentic
Shrugging off those that shake their heads

What's more punk rock
Than simply, fuck you!

We were told
By everyone
That our dreams
Would not amount to much
Or anything at all
But I believed in everything
We did
I still do
Every late-night idea
Every note scribbled down
On hands, paper and napkins
Here and there
Every drunk conversation
Filled with laughter at the thought of us
Finally doing something
And sticking it to them
The second we were brave enough
To take the leap
It was obvious
We had something to offer
A reason to keep on keeping on
Nose to the grindstone
Pushing forward
Whilst everyone else fell behind
I believe wholeheartedly
In us, the misfits
Look at us now
Soaring with wings
We built ourselves
Whilst everybody else was on the ground
Laughing
So like a pigeon in a tree
We shit on them

In the beginning there was me
No wall around me
Just a few loose bricks
On the floor
Building blocks from my own
Self-doubt
Then slowly but surely
The collection grew
Until I was faced with nothing but walls
Rapidly erecting all around me
Closing in
As every bad thing
Added a brand-new brick
Until suddenly it was tall enough
To stop me from being able to look
Over it
Far too high to climb
Far too strong to break myself
So, there I stayed
Tucked away and hidden
Claustrophobic and alone
Inside a tower I hadn't been brave enough
To leave
When I'd had the chance

As if by magic
You happened to come across the tower
Whilst you were running
From your own mistakes
Something made you stop and stare
Filling you with a curiosity
You could not ignore
Driven with a desire to know
What was trapped inside
Unafraid that it could be a monster
You took a hammer to it
And sent it crashing down around me
For the first time in a while
I could breathe again
Vulnerable
But free
A miracle
I basked in the sunlight
I'd been without for so long
Determined to never find myself
Trapped in the tower ever again
Finally
I learnt that you can
(And should)
Take all the time that you need
To find your true self again
To build a refuge
Inside your own mind and
Inside your own heart instead of
Desperately trying to claw yourself
Into somebody else's
It is necessary to build your happy place
And love yourself just as much
As you love the most important people in your life
Because you are worthy of it, too
And you are entitled to
Be a little bit selfish sometimes
Take the time to look at all the cracks,
Dents
And missing pieces
Fix some things
And smile
When you would once have averted your eyes

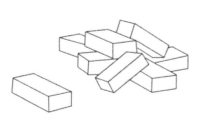

With my heels digging into the soft grass
And my hands looped behind my head
I am happy to leave my mind
Wandering aimlessly
Pleasantly pottering
In and out of reality
Like a summer daydream
A whisky sour on ice beside me
To quench the thirst
I am so easily distracted
By the splatter of fluffy white clouds
Above me
Forming shapes and
Telling stories
For my eyes only
Taken along for the ride, I watch
Mesmerised and intrigued
By the stories in the sky
Herds of animals gather
Chasing each other through the Serengeti
Fighter jets soar
Dogfighting for dominance
Boats and fish and ducks
Head up a stream
And then there is Freddie
Playing something on piano
I can hear the notes so clearly
Inside my own head
And then I notice the gaps of blue
Bright and strong between the chaos
Brought back to reality, I relax
Reminded of your eyes

If heaven and hell
Really do exist
Then you'll find us
Descending in the end
We have never cared enough
To be good at
Avoiding temptation
Spent our whole lives leaning in
To the devil on our shoulders
Listening to his dastardly whispers
Whistles blow
All aboard the train to the underworld
We'll travel in style
And finally we'll fit in
Drinking at the bar
Amongst the misfits and scoundrels
With enough stories of the good ol' days
From living life in the fast lane
To fill the rest of time
Content in the decisions we made
To live freely

The leaves are all but gone
Leaving behind nothing but the
Skeletal body of the trees
The vibrant colours of autumn
Have all faded and dissolved
Into the cold, hard ground beneath our feet
We don our coats and scarfs and gloves
Our armour against the chill
Clouds of breath billow ahead of us
Like the dragon inside is waking up
The sun is lower but somehow brighter
And has no trouble bursting through
The silhouettes
Of naked trees
Reflecting on the snow
In all its glory
Casting a glittering sense of magic
All around us
Breathtaking hues of yellows and reds
Contrast with the dingy greys and browns
As the last of the summer deer
Cross the planes
Ready to hunker down
In shelter
To rest and eat
And in just one frozen moment
I have it all in front of me
A scene from a perfect Christmas card
The stag looks to me
And I, to him
A fleeting look of mutual appreciation
Ready to go our separate ways
Until spring arrives
Melting the snow
And chasing away the winds frosty bite
And it's time to see each other
Again

I look up at the night sky
Mesmerised by the abundance of stars
So close together
Then it hits me and I realise how far apart
They are
And I can't help but wonder if they feel
Lonely up there
It makes me realise that even when they're
Not around
The people I love the most are never that far away
And the stars they're seeing are the stars
I'm seeing
And we're connected not by distance
But by the heart
And by the universe
And suddenly I don't feel lonely anymore
And I hope the stars don't, either

You have survived
All your bad days
And all the dark days
That came before this one
All the trouble that
You have ever been in
All the sleepless nights, the
Countless fights
And terrible frights
You have emerged
Tougher than before
Battered, bruised and scarred
Each one a lesson learnt
But always powering on
You have pulled yourself through the darkest storm clouds
Even when it felt too turbulent to fly
Battle on, soldier
Fight off every dark thought,
Demon and burden
That tries its best
To sneak up on you
And catch you off guard
Remember all the times you've won
And learn from all the times you've lost
Because even then, you bounced back
You have survived
If the darkness surrounds you
And the water starts to rise
And you can't seem to find a way out
Remember how you have braved this fight before
How you swam to safety
How this too, shall pass
How you are never on your own
How through it all
You have survived

Dog days, as they say
Are well and truly here
Party lifestyles
A distant memory
Collectively we've swapped
Our glad rags
For slippers
Our all nighters
For early nights
Our baggies
For bags under the eyes
Now we're the old dogs
With a lot less new tricks
We've grown up
(*Dis*)gracefully
With memories full
Of sore feet from hours of dancing
Sore heads from hours of drinking
A soundtrack of laughter
Floats back to us
With fondness
Together we did it all
Survived the hangovers
The next day sickness
The walks of shame
Mouths like the Sahara
That we would fix
With a hair of the dog
Remember that cloud of regret?
How it would hover above us
Mocking our choices
Now it is a welcome reminder of how
We lived and laughed
Through everything
And bloody hell
Didn't we have fun doing it

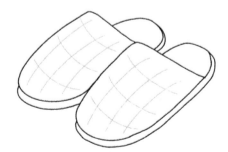

Now here we are
At the end of an adventure
Not completely unscathed
It has to be said
But covered in scars that will always remind us
Of the strength in battle
We had to show
To leave our enemies behind us
Defeated
And no longer giving chase
In front of us now is an open road
Full of uncertainty and fun
A blank canvas
Waiting for our next decisions to make their marks
And there is nothing more beautiful
Than that
Looking forward
Wrapped in love that will always remind us
That we are never truly and completely alone
While we contemplate if we are ready
To start all over again
But knowing that we don't have a choice
Because life is often funny like that
So we take a deep breath
Look at each other and grin
"Race you"

All we have to do now
Is live

Poetry has always felt like a branch of therapy for me. It allows me to sort through whatever emotions I'm feeling at the time, it gives me a way to express myself that feels healthy and natural. And without sounding ridiculously pretentious, it gives my heart a chance to shatter and repair itself over and over again without any cause for concern. It a lifeline that I cling to when I'm upset or angry, it grounds me when I am excited and happy. It is often the only way I know how to voice my feelings, and I am forever grateful to it.

During a time of complete and utter uncertainty, Catharsis was something real and hopeful for me to cling onto and work on whenever I needed it (and my goodness, I needed it. A lot more than I realised; I think).

It was somewhere to channel all the weird and wonderful emotions that I was experiencing, it didn't matter if I was anxious, deeply sad and lonely or going through a sudden outburst of hopefulness and happiness, whatever it was, working on Catharsis provided something solid to continuously come back to and pour my heart into.

Jack and I had been half-heartedly joking about writing a book together for the best part of six years, but we were always far too busy to sit down and actually do it - but when we were all of a sudden faced with far too much spare time thanks to a global pandemic, we knew it was the right time to finally give it a shot. It was now or never, so to say, so we started chucking ideas back and forth until we had a structured idea and then we got stuck in!

William Shakespeare wrote some of his most famous tragedies during the plague and whilst I am definitely not comparing us to Shakespeare (even our egos combined aren't quite that big!) I am still incredibly proud of what we've been able to produce during an awful time, how far we've come and how somehow, we haven't had even one major disagreement throughout the process!

Until I met Jack, I had never written with anybody else, had actually never really wanted to, as writing is often a solitary and personal experience, but writing this book was an incredible experience that has changed me for the better. To be able to do it with a friend bought an entirely new layer of fun to the experience, and definitely lessened the stress (though if you ask Jack, I'm sure he will tell you, there was still a lot of manic stress and panic on my part!).

So in the future, when people ask us how it was to live through this pandemic, we will always have this book to serve as a reminder that even when it was at its worst, when we couldn't see our loved ones, and it felt like there was no way out - we still managed to keep our heads full of ideas, pages full of words and a friendship that allowed us to open our hearts and bleed freely with each other in an open and honest way.

So here's to us, for taking an awful situation and somehow turning it into something we can be proud of.

This really was my catharsis, and my god am I proud of it, and even more so - of us.

To put this time of writing into words, I think it's only fair to pull the lid off what's left of a nice single malt and chuck a couple of whisky stones in a crystal tumbler.

This book was born at the start of a pandemic. Which is nuts when you think about it. The whole world just stopped spinning and was frozen in a type of fear that I've never witnessed before in my life. You couldn't even buy anything in the supermarkets. I mean, what's the deal with someone eating a bat and then people around the world couldn't wipe their arse for weeks?

So, the world goes into lockdown and we decide to write a book. Imagine. We'd talked about it for years but this seemed like the perfect time to sit down and get it done. Not like we could go anywhere anyway. So we began work on something and then the most crazy year and a half passes. While we're tinkering inside the world is going absolutely fucking nuts just outside our windows.

There was WW3, Australia burnt down, America went (more) insane, Harry and Megan left the royal family and absolutely nobody cared. Even Brexit actually happened.

There were UFO sightings, concentration camps, riots, movements and lots and lots of anger for all sorts of different reasons. The world was seemingly brought to its knees and then as if one global pandemic wasn't enough, Ebola decided it was coming back for about a week.

Everything was cancelled and we were all made to sit indoors, working from the spare bedroom, bored, not being able to see our families and friends. Unless you were lucky enough to work in health care, or a supermarket or a school, and got to risk your life because you were essential to keeping the lights on in this dark world. Never had I been happier to be called 'non-essential' in my life. We even went full Hunger Games and got divided into tiers and were told to stay in those boundaries for fear of being arrested.

The world needed help and, almost more importantly, needed a good laugh. So some rednecks stormed the Capital building and a large cargo ship got stuck in the Suez Canal after drawing a dick shaped pattern in the ocean. Absolute banter.

How am I supposed to begin to explain this to my grandkids one day? Fucking biblical. I can see it now, having the 'which lockdown was your favourite lockdown?' conversation when we're old and grey and living in care homes.

So yeah, I guess you could say this book was a superb distraction from the craziness of the world for a while. It gave me time to look inwards and really take stock of what was happening, and what had happened in my life, my heart and my head. And while that was really fucking hard, it truly was my Catharsis during the most bonkers time.

Thank you, Paige, for believing in me and I can't believe we've done it. Book 2?

Printed in Great Britain
by Amazon

84452745R00089